For sentimental souls.

.

Sentimental Health

Dedicated to

Issa, Amanda, Danny and Olie; our home, wherever we are.

Pratap, Shikha, Urmi, Ayan, Parth, my sun, moon, and stars.

Contents

Worldly Unwise

Networking

Who do you know?
Why aren't you trying?
Where are you going?
How will you make it?
When will you learn?

What do I do?

Maybe the reason
I don't like you
is because you see
who I really am
that terrifies me

Whole Foods, Incomplete Funds

That'll be $68.
For 7 items?
The bag is 10 cents.

Minimum Wage

Clock out for lunch,
you've only got your
thirty.

You chug you crunch,
your stomach has been
yearning.

Drink up your cup,
your coffee's full and
burning.

Blow twice or thrice
your tongue has started
hurting.

Clock in from lunch,
you've still got hours
lurking.

Get back to work,
to pennies you are
earning.

Finding Purpose

It was a long road,
that still stretches far.

I didn't know I would get here,
I didn't know my heart.

Where it takes me,
I can never know.

Valleys, cities, changing directions,
every high and low.

Millennialism

Be a #BOSS!
But live in the moment.
Play the field!
But don't be a sl*t.
Do what you love!
But make money.
Travel the world!
But stay humble.
Be a foodie!
But fit and strong.
#Selfie!
Unfollow.

Idle Hands

My mind runs fast,
yet time, slow
I want to do it all
yet nothing at all
I feel worthless
but worthy of
everything
a waste of space
yet taking it up.

Two Cents

Our biggest dreams
often cause us
the most pain.

Yet pain and pleasure exist
on the same coin,
like satisfaction and regret.

Invest wisely,
don't flip
for your future.

PROS | CONS

Binge Thinking

Eat and eat and eat and eat
until it hurts
but why do I
eat and eat and eat and eat
and still feel
empty?

The Moon

Silver waves
Dark waters
Rippled moon
I lifted my eyes to steal a look
He was waiting for me
I felt the gaze
He stared at me all night.

Lostalgia

Old friends, swimming by,
passing in the waves.
Old times, drifting on,
lost to the wind.
New worlds rising,
things yet to be seen.
The present now seems,
loaded with it all.

Second Life

Painted faces,
stuffed crusts,
laughing loudly,
too.

Forgotten homework,
playground gossip,
broken friendships,
you.

College bars,
library books,
feeling lonely,
true.

Rental payments,
wine glasses,
betrayed trust,
blue.

First dates,
awkward silence,
moving in,
I do.

Highchairs,
ABCs,
first steps,
anew.

Career Goals

Adrenaline rushing
Elevator dinging
Click-clacking
Face blushing
Palms sweating
Handshaking
Question asking
Stammering
Panicking
Resume skimming
Door opening
"Thank you for coming in"

Can't sleep, won't sleep.

I know these hurdles
I know this sadness
I have been to this place
before
It is a circle I keep walking
Visiting familiar spots
Nothing changes
but once again
I'll stow it all away until
next time.

Whatever is mine please shine

We All Scream for iScreen

Open, close, reopen
Wait, wonder
Like, comment
Follow

Consuming
Captivated
Scrolling
Enraptured

Are you sure
you want to
deactivate?
Close, Reopen

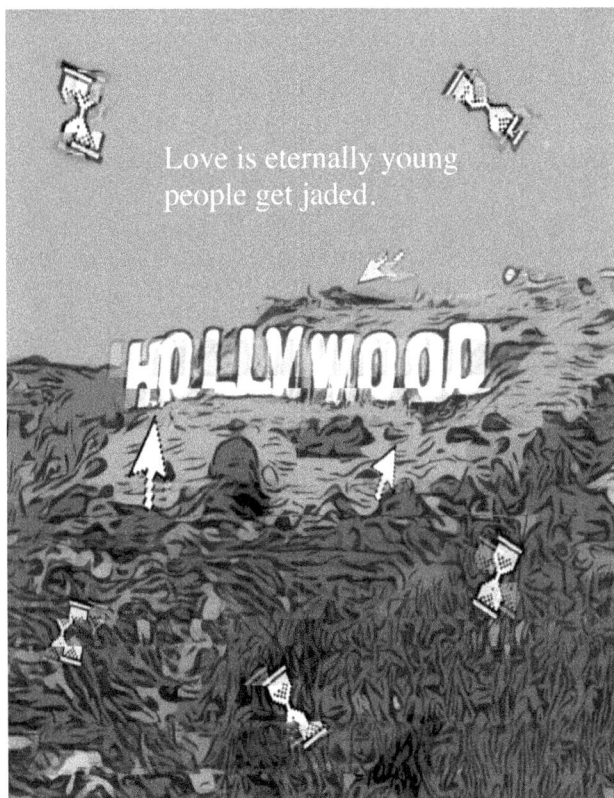

Socially Distanced Relationship

The best thing I can do for you
is stay away.

Blood, Water, Oil

Why is it
the ones
who love
the most
can hurt
the most?

Fair Weather Friend

A friend, you pretend,
yet I want you to like me
you make me feel small,
and hold me so tightly
I wish I could leave
you back in my past
but somehow, I know,
you won't go
till you're asked

"Grow Up"

For a moment,
my cheeks burned,
I'd gone so long
without honesty.

The truth reminds us
to be humble,
but use it carefully.

They are not
sticks or stones
but words may surely
hurt me.

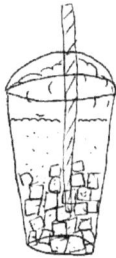

I Left My Heart in Junior School

Betrayed and broken
it's all over now
for everyone
but me

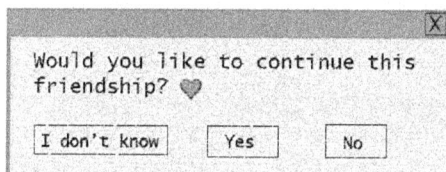

Would you like to continue this friendship? ♥

I don't know | Yes | No

The Weight of The World

Watching the clouds through the skylight,
wisping surprisingly fast.
Thoughts of nothing creep upon me,
how can nothing feel so vast?

So Much for Sisterhood

I can do this
and
I can do that
and
I can do this
better than
she can do that
and

I can't do this.

Lonely Girl

I'd hear people talk about it,
but not me.

Too independent,
I didn't need anyone.

It's different now,
I know what it's like to hold and be held.

I understand now,
they were not lonely for a person, but a feeling.

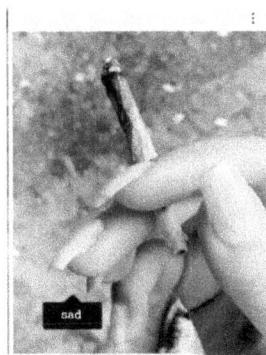

"Must Have Reliable Transportation"

Private Property
Violators will be towed
Street cleaning
Permit only
Fire hydrant
30-minute parking
Valet only
Loading only
Pay to Park
No parking

Panic Attack

Barreling
from a distance
a twister
kettle boiling
floodgates bursting
red
breathless
black
sickness
help
sirens ringing
turbine slowing
breath back
land restoring
colour
river flowing
peace
for now

Location, Location, Location

What is a place without a memory?
What are memories without people?
Perhaps home is not where you hang your hat,
but where your people are.

Body, Mind… Soul?

Mistakes
caught up with me
stupid
lack of discipline
work
extra hard
get
back on track
lose
everything
how
I hate that
girl
in the mirror
how
I long to have her back.

Oppressive Consuming Debilitation

It's got to the point
where my compulsions
have more of a life
than I do.

I Can't Make It Tonight

It's hard not to be depressed,
when you're so f*cking depressed.

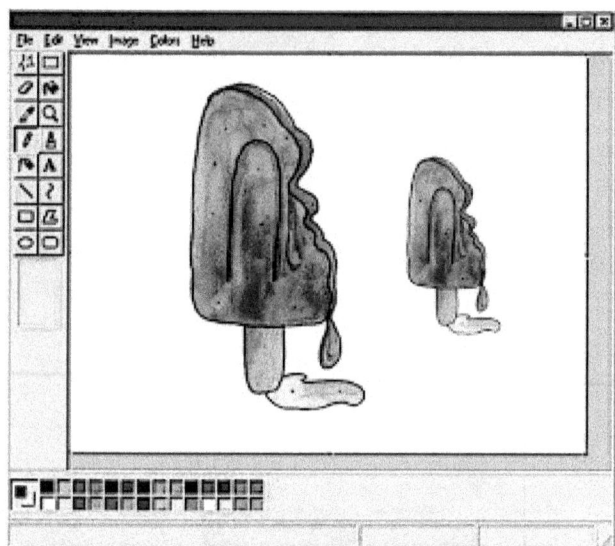

Mean Girls

How I wish I didn't care,
weightless I would be.
Your words, your whispers,
your judging stares.
All I want is to be me.

Help Me Help You

Please stop
destroying
yourself

I can't take
watching you
self-torment

Helpless
fearing I'll
make it worse

Can anyone
help
before I need help myself?

Retail Therapy

Your grimace gave away
when I asked about your day
the longer there you stood
the more I wished you would
have picked another cashier

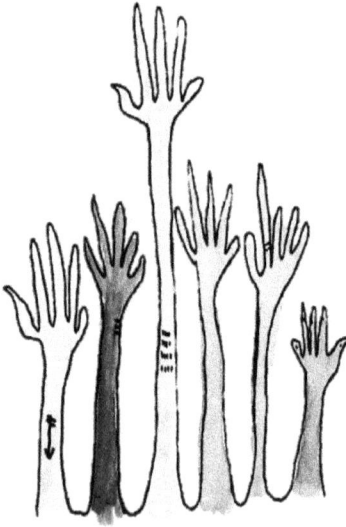

I Name You, OCD

Speak up
you must
or it will
consume you
tell someone
write it down
call it out
or it will fester
speak up now
if you can

Unlucky in Love

Space Is Overrated

It gets worse
with time
I hoped
it would get easier
to forget
not what we were
but what
I wouldn't let us be

Mismatch

I'm so f*cking lonely,
and you're in the other room.

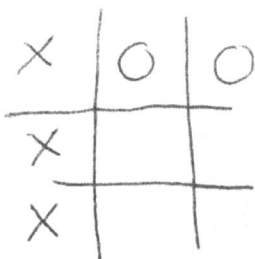

Do I love you?

This blanket keeps me warm,
I reach for it to hold.
But do I need the blanket
if I don't sleep at all?

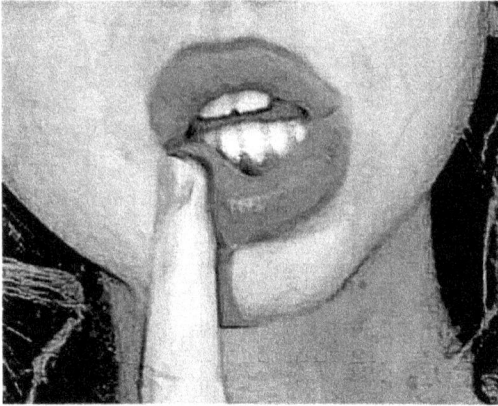

Deafening Silence

Dull agony breeds silence
sharp pains bleed screams
I can't make a sound
at the thought of you.

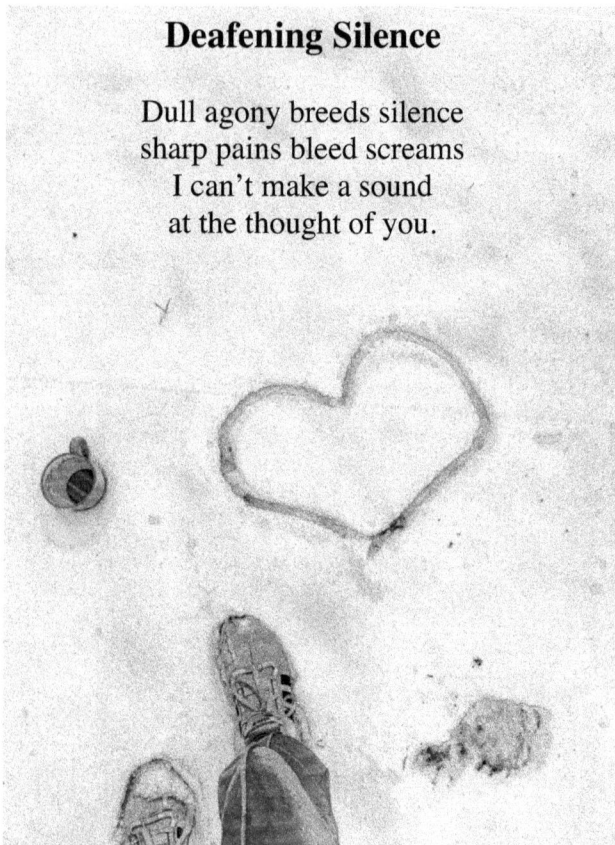

Self-torture

You lie, I know you do,
tell me what I want to hear,
yet I stick around with you
and listen with an open ear.

Sleeping with A Narcissist

It was the little things, too.
"Bring some friends over with you."

The sinking feeling in my stomach.
"You're wrong."

I miss you, but I miss myself more.
Goodbye.

Phantom Feelings

I only remember the ghost of me,
for you have turned me to cinder,
the tombstone ahead of my time.

Drinking About You

One more shot
you'll forget
two more rounds
to be numb
shot it up
chase it down
keep the party going
you can't think about him
if you can't think at all.

Just one more...

Broken Silence

To my surprise,
you forgave me,
I cried in your car for hours.

We walked down the seafront,
below the stars,
unwrapping it all.

You forgot your keys,
we had to walk back,
I ignored the pain in my heels.

You looked at me
with almond eyes,
I felt the swirl within me.

You drove me home
and went your own way,
I will probably love you forever.

Love, Accelerated

We raced down the highway,
fear in our hearts,
love in our veins.

You said to kiss you
before the traffic lights,
I said you were crazy.

Our first kiss,
60mph,
yellow light.

It makes sense now,
as we add up the miles
why we crashed.

Temptation Aisle

Get out of my head
invasive presence
bad for me
like a glazed doughnut
at the counter
I want you
but just for the moment
yes, I'm ready to order.

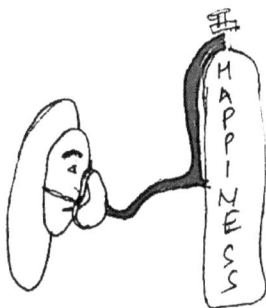

Fool Me Twice

You betray me
in the worst ways
yet here I am
still looking
the other way
I can't even
blame you now
shame on me

Pain, Pain, Go Away

Missing you is like rain,
hitting quietly first,
then pouring, unrelenting,
until the next sunny spell.

I Remember Your Laugh

Best friend,
almost lover,
how you've grown.

I still have
the old you,
at least in memory.

I'll always love you,
but for us,
it is not meant to be.

Oh that attraction!
Oh that uncomfortable familiarity in your face!
I wish you didn't remind me of other people

We are bound like tears
together in pain and pleasure.

You don't need sounds,
you don't need words.
I know what you want to say,
but I will still play.
Twist your sounds,
twist your words.
Why? I ask myself.

With you,
there is space for me
but there is no place for me
And place isn't something one asks for

🖤🖤🖤🖤🖤🖤🖤🖤🖤🖤🖤🖤🖤🖤🖤🖤🖤🖤🖤🖤🖤
🖤🖤🖤🖤🖤🖤🖤🖤🖤🖤🖤
🖤🖤🖤🖤🖤🖤🖤🖤🖤🖤🖤🖤🖤🖤🖤🖤🖤🖤🖤🖤🖤
🖤🖤🖤🖤

I healed myself and forgot to use
my broken heart for art
oh well...next time
🖤🖤🖤🖤🖤🖤🖤
🖤🖤🖤🖤🖤🖤🖤🖤🖤🖤🖤🖤🖤🖤🖤🖤🖤🖤🖤🖤🖤
🖤🖤🖤🖤🖤🖤🖤🖤🖤🖤
🖤🖤🖤🖤🖤🖤🖤

Pull Over

How many red flags,
before you leave a liar behind?
As many as it takes,
until you get off that track.

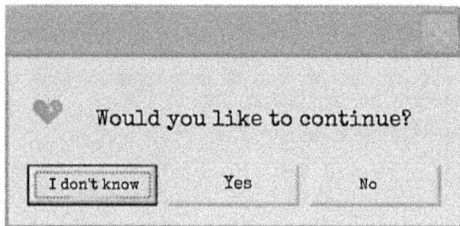

Would you like to continue?

I don't know   Yes   No

Apocalypse, You

Unrecognizable.
Now you are
someone else
who could hurt me

Broken.
You lied
like it was oxygen
I meant less than nothing.

Upturned.
My world
no trust
unable to love anymore.

I spent my day's love on you
then I spent my life's love on you that day.
Your love is what fills my heart anew
Then you ask for all of it to be spent on you
I see how you make me dance
I love this dance
I will dance forever with you

Used

I was a fresh sheet of paper
unblemished and clean
you crumpled me up and
threw me away
unrecycled, unloved

Sugar

Sickly sweet
bad for me
momentary relief
addicted
vicious cycle
I endure
the kid in
your candy store

I Wish You Better Than Me

I see your pictures,
you only post rarely.

You've come into your own,
quirky round sunglasses.

Though you're with her now,
I'm overjoyed.

Because I know you're loved,
the way you deserve.

Codependent

I was
stuck in sand
despair
with less energy

if you hadn't
lent your hand
would I have
moved?

now I am
clinging to you
unhealthy
dragging you down

I am at least
different
closer, but not
unstuck

I fear
life without you
if you go
what will I be?

I know it is
within me
to pull myself
out of the desert

I must
use my own
strength
before I sink.

Brick Wall

You don't ask
about my day
unless it pertains
to something
you need

You don't
communicate or
let me in

I feel as though
I'm lonelier
with you
than when I'm
alone

I want to be happy for you,
but I can't be happy.

Afraid to Love You

Tell me one more story
you always make me laugh
accents and your anecdotes
a blast from the past
but when I disappoint you
you change before my eyes
a shadow of the old you
one I can't recognize

Canary

Canary sees the bars
the world beyond the gaps
her freedom
lies out there.

Owner comes
seed in hand
Canary knows better
yet still, she eats.

Safety, security
within iron bars
but I ask,
what life?

Lying to yourself,
dear Canary,
for you are a woman.
Fly free, before it's too late

Ones That Got Away

Soul, Mate

Answered on the first ring
too desperate perhaps
so long since I'd
heard your voice

Butterflies fluttered
to their old haunt
awkward at first
till we found our feet

It took over
back and forth
I found myself falling
all over again

"Seen"

When I don't reply
it is not you
sometimes
there is already
too much noise
in my mind
to let you in

Stay

Sweetness and salt,
together as one.
One day you won't be here,
I miss you already.

Growing to Love

Waking up with love,
it feels new.
But all along you have
loved me unconditionally.
Thank you for waiting,
sorry I'm late.

I see you when I see myself.
I see myself when I see you.

One New Notification

Butterflies in my
stomach
smile on my
face
like a Christmas
present
I'm anxious to
unwrap
What will it be this
time?
I best wait a
moment

Maybe if I post
one more photo
you'll message
then I can stop
wondering what
you're doing.

Chemistry Vs. Compatibility

It's hard to admit
how excited you make me
I can't pinpoint why

Everything is
heightened in your wake
yet we barely know each other

I should go on
with tried and tested,
though it doesn't excite my body

But perhaps
I've had it wrong
all this time

What if calmness
is the real
stuff of love?

Stood Up in The City

You waited
bars, restaurants
excuses, excuses
then one day
you stopped
your final straw
my missed opportunity

Stringing Us Along

You make me laugh
in a new type of way
I hear your voice in each text.

I'm late to our dates,
take days to reply
yet there you are again.

Something is off,
I can't tell what,
something doesn't fit.

Perhaps I'm lying,
more than I think,
I'm sorry, but this is it.

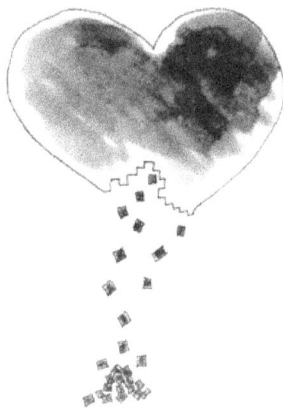

Chapstick On Your Nightstand

You were quiet,
compared to your friends.
I was a curious cat.

We talked over
vodka, soda and lime.
I thought I'd read you like a book.

Who'd have known,
there was such fire inside you?
What a night in Camden Town.

Company, Not Companionship

You stayed the night
we didn't go all the way

a shared shower
conversation till dawn

morning came
couldn't get rid of you

biscuits in bed
pretense overload

we both knew
there was nothing to it

simply two
sparkless university students

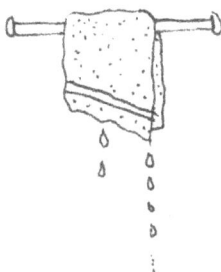

Self-sabotage

You leaned away
from my kiss
I'd gone too far
You mentioned his name
dumped me by text
I was relieved
in a way
You always deserved
better than me.

Love Triangle

What to do with you?
Menace to my mind.
One day tripping over love,
next it's out of sight.
Is it me or is it us?
I cannot be sure.
We have something,
it's just not
that.

Shoulda, Woulda, Coulda

Don't message me
Don't view my story
Don't get in my head
Won't think about you
Won't dream about you
Won't lose my head
Can't not miss you
Can't help but imagine
Can't get you out of my head

Young Thing

What an innocence
you have about you
plate of chips
on your floor
it seems you adore me
you must be blind
yet I enjoy it
though I shouldn't
I must let you go
you have no idea
what I am.

There will be no regret or pleasure bigger than what
happened last night
It was tempting, I held myself back
My eyes locked on his face; a whole millennium passed
It was the moment of decision, move forward of retreat?
I stepped closer; his scent pulled me in
I couldn't resist
There will be no regret or pleasure bigger than what
happened last night.
Whole bag of chips past midnight.
That body, soft to the touch
Enveloping intense aroma
That deafening crunch draining out every other thought
Mmmmm, licking each finger one by one
Reaching deep inside for that last piece
Satisfaction on the face
Oh! that crushing of the empty bag!
There will be no regret or pleasure bigger than what
happened last night.

Working on The Lyrics

Did that just happen?
Or have I been
starved of affection
for so long?
Now comes
the tricky part,
I'm falling for you.

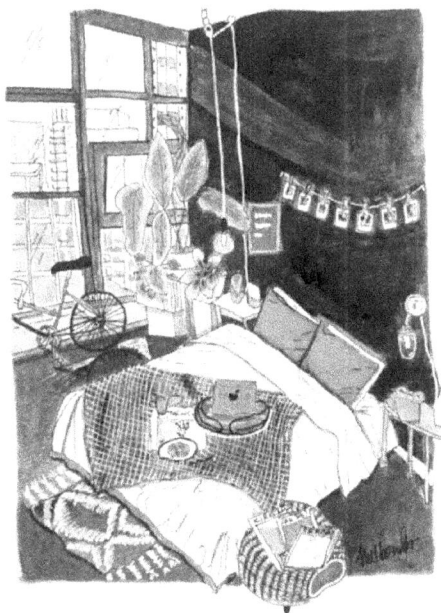

Afterglow

What a blissful affliction,
you.

Like You Never Happened

I can't remember our first kiss
I don't remember your drink
I must have been so wrapped up
in forgetting him
to memorize you

Skin on Skin

Your presence fills me
I never want to
step out of it
lying next to you
there is nothing
more I wish for
than for this moment
to be stretched till eternity

Foreigners

You caught my eye,
beauty in that grey town
one word led to another
kiss at the back
of the bus
blue eyes sparkled
teacher caught us
you told me "Au revoir".

I just want to be
a piece of your day

The First

We built it up
in our minds

the night was electric
like lightning

two sensible teens
we did all the right things

but things changed
age jaded us

yet after all is
said and done

I would do us all
over again.

Special One

We sat
the same
train home
you told me
you put ice
in your cereal
we laughed
about nothing
I didn't know
what it was
but I knew
how I felt
I could see it
but it changes
everything
I'd rather
go on
unknowing
you're too
special
too scary
for me

Gratitude Adjustment

I'm listening

Nothing is better
than a fresh cup of tea
except when it's made
by a friend.

Mum

My light
my flame
my embers
I wish to
be near you
always
your firefly.

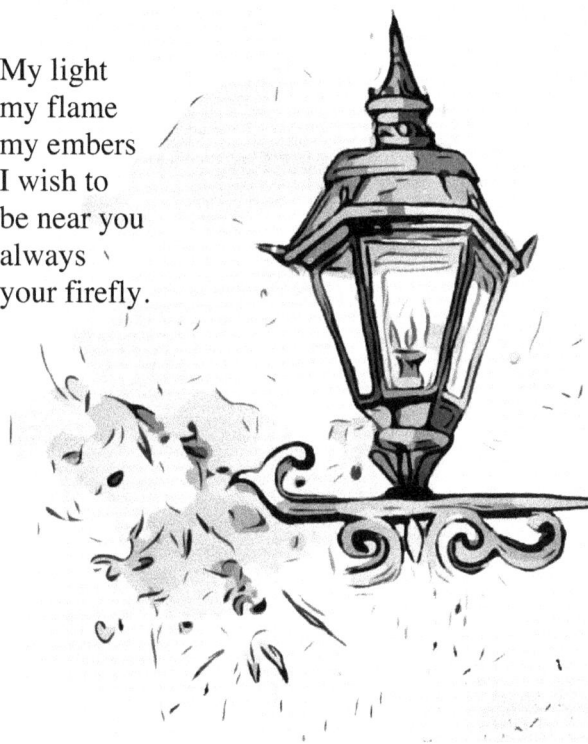

In this void is where I will make my roots
Everything familiar is slipping away
I want to hold on, but it wants to leave
New stands on the horizon, looking me in the eye
I stand still caught in this void where neither new nor
old exists
I stand still making my roots, for I will find myself
here often

Aging Gracefully

Grey hair hello there
you comfort me slightly
silver line there you shine
a reminder
I must use my time wisely

I had to lose a lot to learn to live.

It's Not Always Easy

Breathe.
Check in.
You are okay, in this moment.

Rise above the clouds if you wish to never have a cloudy day again.

She swayed in bliss
as golden wheat ears in
the summer breeze.

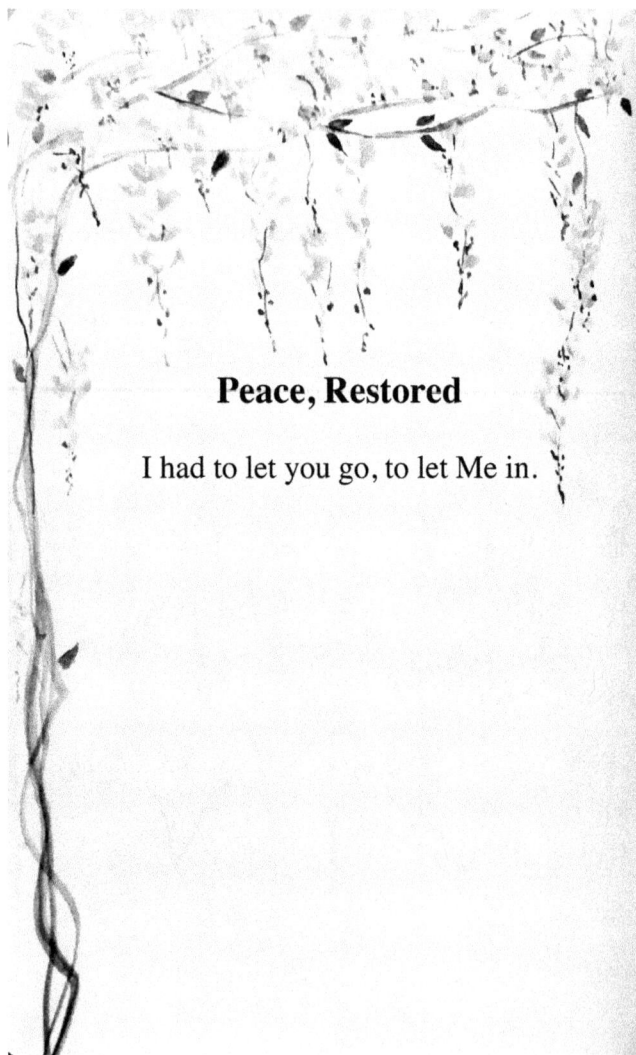

Peace, Restored

I had to let you go, to let Me in.

No one lost is lost,
Earth is round, you'll see them again.

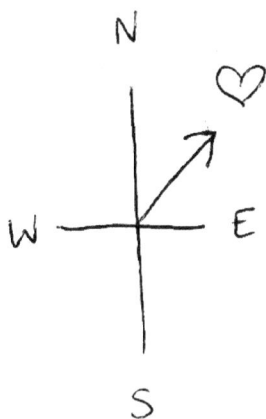

Something Good

When goodness arrives
bathe in it
let it take you over
like sunlight on your skin.

Find Something to Live For

It's okay to fall
and not want
to get up.
But you must
get up.

Get. Up.

Family

Thank God for you
my saving graces
the sad days and wrong ways
lessened

Your love pours
like light through the window
in dawns and dusks
when I don't sleep

Love You, Self

Not anymore, no.
Too much pain, coming from me.
I won't go on that way,
losing myself and others.
I will have good days, I will have bad.
I choose to love myself,
no matter what.

Best Friend

Time, compassion
overflowing love
doing for others
before yourself
constancy, honesty
a well of laughter
proof there is good
in the world.

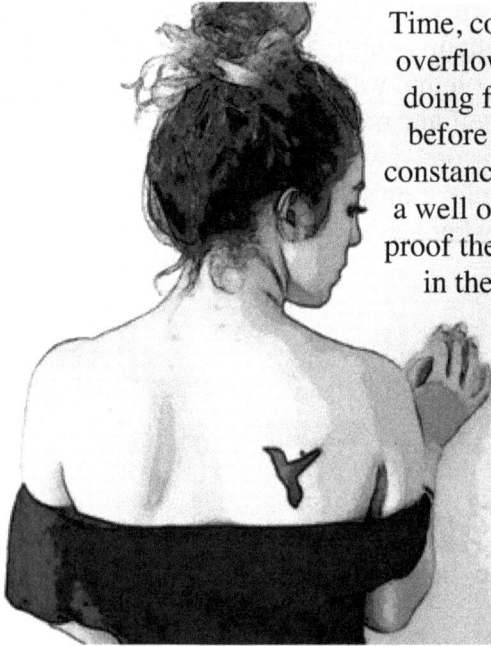

Love of My Life

You smile when you
walk in the room
I can't help but smile back.

The wrinkles
by your eyelids,
lines I've learnt.

Hold me
the way you do,
all the way around.

I'll hold on
to that feeling,
I'll keep smiling for you.

Loosening the Reins

Blind Ambition

Maybe it's OK
to be normal
no fame, fortune
or special recognition

Only normal
whatever that means
maybe it's OK
maybe it's Everything.

```
  G                M
  R                Y
H A    P    P      Y
  T                S
  I                E
  T                
  U              L O V E
  D                F
  E
```

Alone, not Lonely

I have talent
I have depth
I have doubts, sometimes

I have love
I have promise
I get lonely, sometimes

I have strength
I have charm
I have me, always

Twenty Something

Indecisive
Introverted
Individual
Incredible

Independent
Influenced
Insistent
Inspiring

Messy,
in all the right ways.

Nightclub Mirror Mantra

Get out there
Queen
just this once
let yourself be
worries can wait
until tomorrow
tonight, just dance
dance it all away

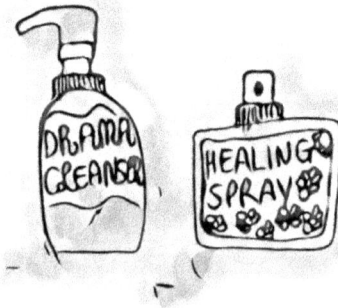

Do It for You

Sing in the car
at midnight
on the quiet roads
dye your hair
if you want to
hope it will grow
embrace heartbreak
because it means
you loved
make a big impression
on yourself

Empath Problems

The world is unfair
things we wish
we could change
but if you let it
consume you
you can't help at all
start small
you are doing
your best.

Magic Song

Smoke drifting
hazing the room
lights flashing
red and green
rhythm lifting
all our feet
liquid over ice
cold and crispy
Her dancing
like she'd
written it

Prom

Broken plastic chair
Out of tune guitar
Sun creeping over the ocean

Heavy eyelids
Torn tuxedos
Dresses getting dusty

Memories everlasting
Exhausted satisfaction
You singing "Hallelujah"

Claim That Sh*t

In this moment
exultation
something
just for you
now you know
you are capable
nothing can
take it away
you did this
this moment
is yours

There's Gotta Be a Better Way

A few drags
enough
to forget it all
for a second

It scared me
finally
an escape
I could turn to

I want better
for myself
to face
the hard going

I guess that means
I'm learning
I guess it means
I'm growing

Home

The
way the living room smelled
piano in the corner
bags of tea mum collected
broken fridge light

Us
singing in the car
gossiping like hens
ordering pizza
laughing till sunrise

What
luck we had to have it all
fun we had each day
love emanated from that house
I'd give to be there now

Sweet Sixteen

Older group around the back
Boy too young to be there
My dress too short
DJ spinning Ne-Yo
Friend lost her virginity
Another needed painkiller
Police car drove by
Parents calling
Birthday girl frantic
Gifts piled in the corner
Heck of a party they said
Rich chocolate cake
"Happy birthday to you"
But what did I wish for,
when I had it all?

Short Term Goals

1. Be okay again.

Call Nature Back

Out of the window
birds still fly
trees still sway
grass still grows

Here we are
within our walls
locked in our minds
distanced

Let's go outside
feel the world
even if
we cannot touch it

What she said.

I lose myself in life
I find myself in music.

Treat the Cause, Not the Symptoms

When you feel
you have no control

you will look for it
elsewhere

be careful
what you find

it may end up
controlling you too.

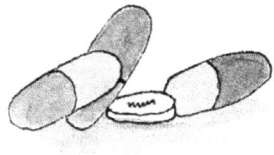

Advice from A Loved One

Let go of the past,
you cannot
change it.

You can change
your behaviour
for the future.

Start now,
in the present,
it's a gift, after all.

About the Authors

Amber Loutfi is a British/Syrian writer and actor based between London and the US. She grew up in Kuwait and studied biology and screenwriting at university. She is passionate about human rights, mental health awareness and women's empowerment. She loves to bake, attend comedy shows and raise her Labrador Retriever and three chickens.

Isabella Loutfi is a British/Syrian illustrator and graphic designer, based in London. She also grew up in Kuwait, is trained in hair styling and makeup, and is an experienced photographer. She is passionate about health and fitness, mental health awareness and preserving the arts. She enjoys city photography and is a maths enthusiast.

Neeltarni Pratap is Indian/American actor, writer and illustrator, based between Delhi and the US. She is a champion for animal rights and the preservation of the environment. She enjoys caring for her clowder; Pushkin, Shifu, Lulu, Butter and Goji, filmmaking and creating artwork for her online store. She makes hand-poured vegan candles and is a big fan of vegan cake.

Credits

Amber Loutfi
Poems written (page no.): 10,11,12,13, 14, 15, 16, 17, 18, 20, 21, 22, 23, 26, 28, 29
30, 31, 32, 34, 25, 36, 37, 38, 39, 40, 41, 42, 43, 44, 45, 47, 48, 49, 50, 51, 52, 53, 54, 55, 56, 57, 58, 59, 60, 66, 67, 69, 70, 71
72, 73, 74, 75, 76, 78, 79, 80, 81, 83, 84, 85, 86, 87, 88, 89, 90
91, 92, 93, 95, 96, 97, 98, 99, 100, 101, 102, 104, 105, 107, 109
112, 114, 115, 116, 117, 118, 119, 121, 122, 123, 124, 125, 126
127, 128, 129, 130, 131, 132, 133, 134, 135, 137, 138

Poems illustrated: 13, 17, 19, 23, 28, 31, 40, 48, 50, 59, 61, 62, 73, 75, 80, 93,102, 106, 108, 110, 113, 121

Isabella Loutfi
Poems Illustrated: 11, 14, 16, 20, 21, 27, 30, 32, 33, 34, 35, 36, 39, 41, 42, 43, 45, 49, 51, 52, 53, 54, 56, 64, 66, 67, 72, 78, 79, 82, 83, 84, 85
88, 90, 92, 100, 104, 117, 118, 119, 124, 126, 132, 133, 134, 135, 136, 138

Illustrations edited: 10,12, 15, 18, 22, 47, 60, 87, 105, 107, 114, 116, 123

Neeltarni Pratap
Poems Written: 19, 24, 25, 27, 33, 61, 62, 63, 64, 65, 68, 82, 94, 98, 106, 108, 110, 111, 113, 136

Poems illustrated: 10,12, 15, 18, 22, 24, 25, 26, 29, 37, 38, 44, 47, 55, 57, 58, 60
63, 65, 68, 69, 70, 71, 74, 76, 81, 86, 87, 89, 91, 94, 95, 96, 97
99, 101, 105, 107, 109, 111, 112, 114, 115, 116, 122, 123, 125
127, 128, 129, 130, 131, 137